Illustrated by Pete Avdoulos, Mark Busacca, Emi Fukawa, Victor Lee, Wendy K. Lee, Douglas Scott, Peggy Smith, Alexandr Stolin, Vadim Vahrameev, Hanako Wakiyama, Nelson Wang and Bill Yenne.

Printed in Italy

Series UPC: 39440

Bible Classics

The Story of Jonah

Modern Publishing
A Division of Unisystems, Inc.
New York, New York 10022
Series UPC: 39440

Long ago, there was a great city called Nineveh. It was a large city with many people living in it. God was not pleased because the people of Nineveh did not obey Him.

God decided to send a man named Jonah as a prophet to tell the people of Nineveh to repent.

Because Jonah didn't want to do what God asked, he ran away. He found a ship about to sail to Tarshish, a place far away to the west. He paid the fare and got on board.

Jonah should have known that he could not hide from God or His commands. God caused a great wind to blow across the water.

Huge waves threatened to sink the ship. Jonah was sound asleep when the storm came, but the ship's captain woke him up. He told Jonah to ask God to make the storm stop.

The sailors wanted to know why God was so angry. Jonah told them how he had disobeyed God's command. The sailors were afraid and angry at Jonah for putting them in danger.

They tried to row the ship, but they couldn't. They asked Jonah what they should do. Jonah told them to throw him overboard.

They threw Jonah overboard into the sea. The storm stopped and the water became calm. The Lord did not want Jonah to drown. When Jonah was thrown into the water, he was swallowed by a whale!

It was dark inside the whale. Jonah was scared.
He prayed to God for three days and three nights.

Then God told the whale to spit Jonah out on the coast near Nineveh.

God again asked Jonah to go and warn the people of Nineveh that they must obey Him. This time Jonah did as God commanded.

Jonah told the people of Nineveh that they had to live according to God's laws. If they didn't, in forty days God was going to destroy their city.

Jonah didn't like the people of Nineveh. Still, he preached to them and the people believed. They prayed to God and God forgave them.

Jonah was angry at God for forgiving the people of Nineveh. He thought God should punish them.

He went into the mountains and camped on a spot where he could wait to see if God changed His mind. It was very hot in the mountains.

God took pity on Jonah and made a plant grow where Jonah was sitting. The leaves shaded Jonah from the hot sun. Jonah was thankful for the plant.

That night, God sent a worm to make the plant wither and die. The next day, the sun rose, the wind blew and it was even hotter than the day before.

Jonah had not made the plant grow, but he was angry because it died.

God said, "I gave the plant life, like I gave the people of Nineveh life. I care about what happens to them."

Jonah was no longer miserable and angry at God or the people of Nineveh.

He knew that God loves and cares for everyone who obeys Him.